LEADER GUIDE

A STUDY IN THE BOOK OF JAMES

THRIVE

Living
Faithfully in
Difficult Times

JENNIFER COWART

Abingdon Women/Nashville

Thrive
Living Faithfully in Difficult Times
Leader Guide

ISBN 978-1-7910-2779-7

MANUFACTURED IN THE UNITED STATES OF AMERICA

Contents

ABOUT THE AUTHOR

Jennifer Cowart is the executive and teaching pastor at Harvest Church in Warner Robins, Georgia, which she and her husband, Jim, began in 2001. With degrees in Christian education, counseling, and business, Jen oversees a wide variety of ministries and enjoys doing life and ministry with others. As a gifted Bible teacher, Jen brings biblical truth to life through humor, authenticity, and everyday application. She is the author of three women's Bible studies (*Pursued*, *Fierce*, and *Messy People*) and several small group studies coauthored with her husband, Jim, including *The One*, *Grounded in Prayer* and *Living the Five*. They love doing life with their kids, Alyssa, Josh, Andrew, and Hannah.

Follow Jen:

jimandjennifercowart

jimandjennifer.cowart

Website: jennifercowart.org or jimandjennifercowart.org

Join Jen Cowart
for a one-of-a-kind study experience!

As Bible teacher and life-long learner, Jen loves to connect with other women studying the Bible and exploring faith. She offers a virtual drop in visit for groups studying *Thrive* or her other women's Bible studies.

Whether you're just starting the first session and would love some inspiration straight from the author or you've spent several weeks together in this experience, Jen invites you to contact her directly through email at Jennifer@harvestchurch4u.org to see what can be arranged!

Don't miss this opportunity to connect with an inspiring author and dive deeper into what it means to truly *Thrive*.

INTRODUCTION

Welcome to *Thrive*, a six-week study in the Book of James. *Thrive* describes something alive, vibrant, and moving in the right direction. It means to prosper or flourish. Whether that describes life for you in this season or sounds like wishful thinking because life is hard and you're struggling to get through each day, this study is for you. The purpose of this study is to help you and the women in your group discover that it's possible to thrive at all times regardless of your circumstances!

This letter written in the first century to believers who lived in a climate of persecution is filled with practical instructions about how to endure hardships and move beyond surviving to thriving. Because James's practical instructions often jump from one topic to another, making it challenging to move fluidly through the letter, we will do some intentional bobbing and weaving as we focus on selected verses according to six key themes or habits:

1. Endurance
2. Wisdom
3. Action
4. Control
5. Humility
6. Prayer

ABOUT THE PARTICIPANT BOOK

Before the first session, you will want to distribute copies of the participant workbook to the members of your group. Be sure to communicate that they are to complete the first week of readings before your first group session. For each week there is a Scripture memory verse and five devotional lessons that combine study of Scripture with personal reflection and application. On average, each lesson can be completed in about twenty to thirty minutes. Completing these readings each week will prepare the women for the discussion and activities of the group session.

ABOUT THIS LEADER GUIDE

As you gather each week with the members of your group, you will have the opportunity to watch a video, discuss and respond to what you're learning, and pray together. You will need access to a television and a DVD player with working remotes. Or, if you prefer, you may purchase streaming video files at www.Cokesbury.com, or you may access the videos for this study and other Abingdon Women Bible studies on AmplifyMedia.com through an individual or church membership.

This leader guide and the video lessons will be your primary tools for leading each group session. In this book you will find outlines for six group sessions, each formatted for either a 60-minute or 90-minute group session:

60-Minute Format

Leader Prep (Before the Session)	
Welcome and Opening Prayer	5 minutes
Icebreaker	5 minutes
Video	20 minutes
Group Discussion	25 minutes
Closing Prayer	5 minutes

90-Minute Format

Leader Prep	(Before the Session)
Welcome and Opening Prayer	5–10 minutes
Icebreaker	5 minutes
Video	20 minutes
Group Discussion	35 minutes
Deeper Conversation	15 minutes
Closing Prayer	5 minutes

As you can see, the 90-minute format is identical to the 60-minute format but allows more time for the welcome/opening prayer and group discussion plus a

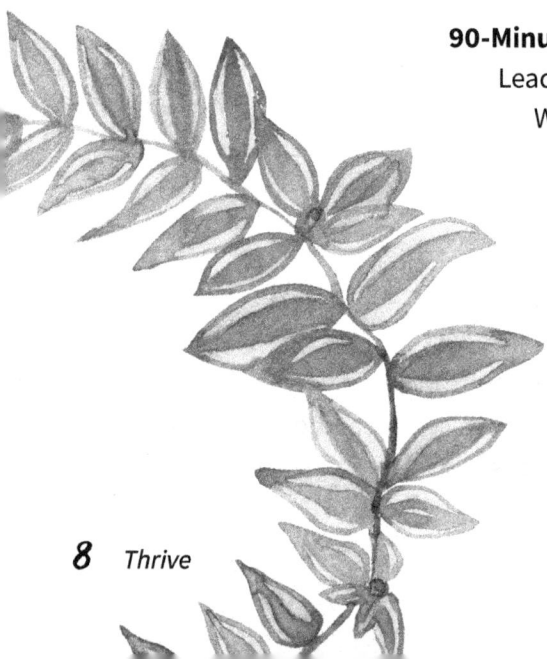

Deeper Conversation exercise for small groups. Feel free to adapt or modify either of these formats, as well as the individual segments and activities, in any way to meet the specific needs and preferences of your group.

Here is a brief overview of the elements included in both formats:

Leader Prep (Before the Session)

For your preparation prior to the group session, this section provides an overview of the week's biblical theme, and a list of materials and equipment needed. Be sure to review this section, as well as read through the *entire* session outline, before your group time in order to plan and prepare. If you choose, you also may find it helpful to watch the video lesson in advance.

Welcome and Opening Prayer
(5–10 minutes, depending on session length)

Create a warm, welcoming environment as the women are gathering before the session begins. Consider lighting one or more candles, providing coffee or other refreshments, and/or playing worship music. (Bring an iPod, smartphone, or tablet and a portable speaker if desired.) Be sure to provide nametags if the women do not know one another or you have new participants in your group. Then, when you are ready to begin, open the group in prayer before you begin your time.

You also may find it helpful to read aloud the week's Overview found in the Leader Prep section if not all group members have completed their homework.

Icebreaker (5 minutes)

Use the icebreaker to briefly engage the women in the topic while helping them feel comfortable with one another.

Video (20 minutes)

Next, watch the week's video segment together. Be sure to direct participants to the Video Viewer Guide in the participant workbook, which they may complete as they watch the video. (Answers are provided on page 60 of this guide and page 201 in the participant workbook.)

Group Discussion (25–35 minutes, depending on session length)

After watching the video, choose from the questions provided to facilitate group discussion (questions are provided for both the video segment and the participant workbook material). For the participant workbook portion, you may choose to read aloud the discussion points or express them in your own words; then use one or more of the questions that follow to guide your conversation.

Note that more material is provided than you will have time to include. Before the session, select what questions you want to ask, putting a check mark beside them in your book. Reflect on each question and make some notes in the margins to share during your discussion time. Page references are provided for those questions that relate to specific questions or activities in the participant workbook. For these questions, invite group members to turn in their books to the pages indicated. Participants will need Bibles in order to look up various supplementary Scriptures.

Depending on the number of women in your group and the level of their participation, you may not have time to cover everything you have selected, and that is okay. Rather than attempting to bulldoze through, follow the Spirit's lead and be open to where the Spirit takes the conversation. Remember that your role is not to have all the answers but to encourage discussion and sharing.

Deeper Conversation (15 minutes)

If your group is meeting for 90 minutes, use this exercise for deeper sharing in small groups, dividing into groups of two or three. This is a time for women to share more intimately and build connections with one another. (Encourage the women to break into different groups each week.) Give a two-minute warning before time is up so that the groups may wrap up their discussion.

Closing Prayer (5 minutes)

Close by leading the group in prayer. If you'd like, invite the women to briefly name prayer requests. To get things started, you might share a personal request of your own. As women share their requests, model for the group by writing each request in your participant workbook, indicating that you will remember to pray for them during the week.

As the study progresses, you might encourage members to participate in the Closing Prayer by praying out loud for one another and the requests given. Ask the women to volunteer to pray for specific requests, or have each woman pray for the woman on her right or left. Make sure name tags are visible so that group members do not feel awkward if they do not remember someone's name.

BEFORE YOU BEGIN

I have spent far too many days of my life in survival mode. Those seasons are tough, and it's not a very fun way to live. Instead, I want to thrive—don't you?

Friend, you have the incredible opportunity to lead others on an exciting journey toward thriving in all circumstances. Your role is not to have all the answers but simply to offer acceptance, compassion, and encouragement along the way. Take a moment now to thank God for this privilege and to ask for guidance, wisdom, and patience for the journey. May you and the women in your group get so close to Jesus that you can face whatever comes your way with the attitude that you are going to thrive! I'm praying for you and cheering you on.

Let's thrive,

Jen

LEADER HELPS

PREPARING FOR THE SESSIONS

- Decide whether you will use the 60-minute or 90-minute format. Be sure to communicate dates and times to participants in advance.
- Ensure that participants receive their workbooks at least one week before your first session and instruct them to complete the first week's devotional lessons. If you have the phone numbers or email addresses of your group members, send out a reminder and a welcome.
- Check out your meeting space before each group session (or set up a virtual meeting and share the link). Make sure the room is ready. Do you have enough chairs? Do you have the equipment and supplies you need? (See the list of materials needed in each session outline.)
- Pray for your group and each group member by name. Ask God to work in the life of every woman in your group.
- Read and complete the week's devotional lessons in the participant workbook and review the session outline in the leader guide. Select the discussion points and questions you want to cover and make some notes in the margins to share in your discussion time.

LEADING THE SESSIONS

- Personally welcome and greet each woman as she arrives (whether in person or online). You might want to have a sign-up list for the women to record their names and contact information.
- At the start of each session, ask the women to turn off or silence their cell phones (or eliminate other distractions if meeting online).
- Always start on time. Honor the time of those who are punctual.
- Encourage everyone to participate fully, but don't put anyone on the spot. Be prepared to offer a personal example or answer if no one else responds at first.
- Communicate the importance of completing the weekly devotional lessons and participating in group discussion.
- Facilitate but don't dominate. Remember that if you talk most of the time, group members may tend to listen rather than engage. Your task is to encourage conversation and keep the discussion moving.
- If someone monopolizes the conversation, kindly thank her for sharing and ask if anyone else has any insights.
- Try not to interrupt, judge, or minimize anyone's comments or input.
- Remember that you are not expected to be the expert or have all the answers. Acknowledge that all of you are on this journey together, with the Holy Spirit as your leader and guide. If issues or questions arise that you don't feel equipped to handle or answer, talk with the pastor or a staff member at your church.
- Don't rush to fill the silence. If no one speaks right away, it's okay to wait for someone to answer. After a moment, ask, "Would anyone be willing to share?" If no one responds, try asking the question again a different way—or offer a brief response and ask if anyone has anything to add.

- Encourage good discussion, but don't be timid about calling time on a particular question and moving ahead. Part of your responsibility is to keep the group on track. If you decide to spend extra time on a given question or activity, consider skipping or spending less time on another question or activity in order to stay on schedule.
- End on time. If you are running over, give members the opportunity to leave if they need to. Then wrap up as quickly as you can.
- Thank the women for coming and let them know you're looking forward to seeing them next time.
- Be prepared for some women to want to hang out and talk at the end. If you need everyone to leave by a certain time, communicate this at the beginning of the group session. If you are meeting in a church during regularly scheduled activities, be aware of nursery closing times.

Endurance

Embracing Obstacles as a Means to Maturity

Session Notes: WEEK 1

_____

_____

_____

_____

_____

_____

_____

_____

_____

_____

_____

_____

_____

_____

_____

_____

_____

LEADER PREP (BEFORE THE SESSION)

Overview

This week we looked at selected verses in the first chapter of the Book of James, along with additional scriptures, as we considered how obstacles can help us to mature spiritually. We considered that we all have seasons filled with difficulties and doubt, as well as joy. But like the first-century believers who endured persecution, we can learn to view our difficulties as opportunities to draw close to the Lord.

Memory Verse:

Dear brothers and sisters, when troubles of any kind come your way, consider it an opportunity for great joy. For you know that when your faith is tested, your endurance has a chance to grow.

(James 1:2-3)

What You Will Need

- *Thrive* DVD and DVD player, or equipment to stream the video online
- Bible and *Thrive* participant workbook for reference
- Markerboard or chart paper and markers (optional)
- Stick-on name tags and markers (optional)
- iPod, smartphone, or tablet and portable speaker (optional)
- Various versions of the Bible, including The Message Bible

SESSION OUTLINE

Welcome and Opening Prayer
(5–10 minutes, depending on session length)

In order to create a warm, welcoming environment as the women are gathering before the session begins, consider lighting one or more candles, providing coffee or other refreshments, playing worship music, or all of these. (Bring an iPod, smartphone, or tablet and a portable speaker if desired.) Be sure to provide name tags if the women do not know one

another or you have new participants in your group. Then, when you are ready to begin, open the group in prayer.

If meeting online, welcome each participant as she joins and encourage the women to talk informally until you are ready to open the group in prayer.

Icebreaker (5 minutes)

Invite the women to share short responses to the following questions:

- What is a difficult experience you encountered in the past? or
- What is a difficult experience you have encountered recently?

Video (20 minutes)

Play the Week 1 video segment. Invite participants to complete the Video Viewer Guide for Week 1 in the participant workbook as they watch (page 40).

Group Discussion (25–35 minutes, depending on session length)

Note: More material is provided than you will have time to include. Before the session, select what you want to cover.

VIDEO DISCUSSION QUESTIONS

- Jen speaks about what Proverbs meant to her as a young person. What similarities do you see between the collection of advice in Proverbs and the advice that James is writing for believers? What differences?
- What does the idea that Jesus had siblings add to your understanding of his experiences and life?
- James offers practical wisdom for life's tough seasons. As you read this week, what seasons and circumstances came to mind for you as a 21st century Christian?
- In this video, Jen underscores that it's not "if" trouble comes to us but "when". Did you find reassurance from James's words that "when your faith is tested, your endurance has a chance to grow" or concern?
- What did you hear in Jen's video that will stay with you this week?

PARTICIPANT WORKBOOK DISCUSSION QUESTIONS

1. In Day 1 of our study we were challenged to recall who introduced us to Jesus for the first time. Some of us were in a church building hearing stories about Jesus from a Sunday school teacher or pastor, and some of us heard about Jesus through a family member, teacher, coach, neighbor, or friend. Meeting Jesus changed our lives—whether immediately or over time.

   • Share who introduced you to Jesus for the first time. (page 14)

   • What do you think it would have been like to be one of Jesus's siblings? (page 14)

   • James overcame his doubts regarding who Jesus was. What doubts have you struggled with in your own faith journey? (page 15)

   • At the end of Day 1, you prayed for a fresh desire to seek Jesus as never before. How is God answering that prayer?

2. During Day 2 of our study, we focused on thriving instead of surviving. After surviving the days and months during the pandemic, we can all agree that our quest is to thrive. We all want the transforming joy that comes when we go from surviving to thriving!

   • When have you experienced a difficult season of life, and what was your first reaction to it? (page 19)

   • As you look back on that difficult time, what did you learn from it? (page 21) How were you changed by that experience?

   • Has there been a difficult season when you turned to the Lord for peace and help? If so, share how that time affected your faith in God. (page 21)

- How has James 1:2-3 brought you comfort and reassurance?

3. On Day 3 we were reminded of disappointments, adversity, and ways we responded to these challenging days.
   - When has life not turned out as you dreamed? When that happened, what was your first response? (page 25)
   - What are some ways God has comforted you during difficult seasons? (page 27)
   - How has God's comfort prepared you to comfort others? (page 27)

4. During our Day 4 lesson we focused on ways to embrace obstacles as a means to maturity in our daily walk with God.
   - Read Psalm 34:18 silently or aloud. What does this passage tell you about God's attitude toward your wounds? (page 30)
   - Ask someone to read aloud James 1:2-4 from The Message Bible (page 28). What does James say will be the outcome of this test? (page 30) Now, reflect on your own life. When have you been in the refiner's fire? What did God produce in your character through this time? (page 31)
   - Why is it important for us to reach out to others during their difficult seasons of life? How might you turn the pain of your past into a ministry to others? (page 32)

5. During our Day 5 lesson we looked at the Scriptures through an eternal perspective. Sometimes it is difficult to focus on the eternal perspective during our day-to-day living.
   - If you could go back and give your younger self some advice regarding difficult times, what would you tell her? (page 37)
   - Troubles are a part of our lives. How did you paraphrase 1 Peter 4:12-13? (page 38)
   - Why is it essential to pray during your good times and not-so-good times?

- How did you paraphrase Revelation 21:4? (page 38) Why is it essential to choose joy? What helps you to do that?

Deeper Conversation (15 minutes)

Divide into smaller groups of two to three for deeper conversation. (Encourage the women to break into different groups each week.) If you'd like, before the session, write on a markerboard or chart paper the questions below. You also could do this in the form of a handout.

- Every struggle in life is an opportunity. How can you invite God into the midst of each situation? How are you going to allow God to produce in you a work that develops character?
- Where did you see God at work in your life this past week?

Closing Prayer (5 minutes)

Close the session by taking personal prayer requests from group members and leading the group in prayer. As you progress to later weeks in the study, you might encourage members to participate by praying out loud for one another and the requests given.

WISDOM

Having Heavenly Perspective on Earthly Issues

Session Notes: WEEK 2

_____
_____
_____
_____
_____
_____
_____
_____
_____
_____
_____
_____
_____
_____
_____

LEADER PREP (BEFORE THE SESSION)

Overview

In our second week of study we focused on the theme of wisdom, reading selected verses in James 1 and 3 as well as additional Scriptures. We saw that God is the giver of true wisdom and wants to give us His insight. In Jeremiah 29:13 we read these words, "You will seek me and find me when you seek me with all your heart." Seeking wisdom from God and godly people equips us to live faithfully and humbly and walk in fellowship with God. With wisdom we are able to see circumstances from God's perspective and discern how God wants us to live.

Memory Verse

> *If any of you lacks wisdom, you should ask God, who gives generously to all without finding fault, and it will be given to you.*
>
> (James 1:5 NIV)

What You Will Need

- *Thrive* DVD and DVD player, or equipment to stream the video online
- Bible and *Thrive* participant workbook for reference
- Markerboard or chart paper and markers (optional)
- Stick-on name tags and markers (optional)
- iPod, smartphone, or tablet and portable speaker (optional)

SESSION OUTLINE

Welcome and Opening Prayer
(5–10 minutes, depending on session length)

In order to create a warm, welcoming environment as the women are gathering before the session begins, consider lighting one or more candles, providing coffee or other refreshments, playing worship music, or all of these. (Bring an iPod, smartphone, or tablet and a portable speaker if desired.) Be sure to provide name tags if the women do not know one

another or you have new participants in your group. Then, when you are ready to begin, open the group in prayer.

If meeting online, welcome each participant as she joins and encourage the women to talk informally until you are ready to open the group in prayer.

Icebreaker (5 minutes)

Invite the women to share short responses to one of the following questions:

- Think of the wisest person you know. If you could ask this person for advice today, what would you ask? or
- What's the best advice you have received from a wise person?

Video (20 minutes)

Play the Week 2 video segment. Invite participants to complete the Video Viewer Guide for Week 2 in the participant workbook as they watch (page 73).

Group Discussion (25–35 minutes, depending on session length)

Note: More material is provided than you will have time to include. Before the session, select what you want to cover.

VIDEO DISCUSSION QUESTIONS

- The memory verse this week says that any who ask God for wisdom will be given wisdom. What do you think is involved in really asking God for wisdom?
- Jen mentions several life areas from friendships to family to finances. Where in your life today do you feel you need the most wisdom?
- The memory verse also uses the descriptor "generously" in how God grants wisdom. How do you see God's generosity in sharing wisdom?
- Who in your own faith life exampled real wisdom to you?

Participant Workbook Discussion Questions

1. This week we explored the meaning of God's wisdom and how it impacts our daily lives. The Bible says that true wisdom is the thing we should all seek. In the books of James and Proverbs we find numerous instructions on how to live.

    *   How might seeking wisdom impact your life? (page 44)
    *   Say the memory verse, James 1:5 (NIV), aloud as a group. According to James, how do we obtain wisdom? (page 46)
    *   Whom do you consider wise? What sets them apart from others? (page 46)
    *   What happens when people rely on their own desires and intellect instead of turning to God for wisdom and discernment?

2. Daily we are confronted with advertisements telling us we need to acquire more and more things. In our Day 2 lesson we read a powerful verse that challenges that desire to want more things: "How much better to get wisdom than gold, and good judgment than silver!" (Proverbs 16:16). In order to live faithfully, we need the wisdom of God.

    *   Read aloud 1 Kings 4:29, 34. What are we told that God gave Solomon, and what happened as a result? (page 50)
    *   In what areas of your life do you need wisdom right now? (page 51)
    *   Reflect on James 1:5-7. When asking God for wisdom, why is it important to ask in faith without doubting God?

3. On Day 3 we focused on the idea that discovering God's perspective is the avenue to finding true wisdom.

    *   Reflect on the opening words of Solomon from Ecclesiastes 1:2-3, 8.
    *   What strikes you about Solomon's observation? Have you ever had similar thoughts? (page 55)

- What can you do to prioritize your relationship with Jesus on a daily basis? (page 57)
- Read aloud Ecclesiastes 12:13-14 and James 3:13. On what do James and Solomon agree? (See page 58.)
- How does reflecting on Jesus lead you toward a life of wisdom?

4. During our Day 4 lesson we were challenged to think about God's will for our lives. We discovered that we should know God personally, love and obey Him, and share Him with others.
   - Is prayer your first reaction or last resort when faced with a decision? What in your approach to prayer needs to change in order for you to seek God with all your heart? (page 63)
   - When seeking God's will for your life, why is it vital to study the Bible?
   - As you seek advice from others, why should you be careful to select mature believers?
   - What does it look like in your life to dwell in God's peace? (page 66)

5. This week we had an opportunity to discover where our faith is lacking as we encounter difficulties and struggles. No matter what happens in our lives, we know God is with us and wants us to seek Him for help.
   - Ask someone to read aloud James 1:2-4. According to James, why are we to consider difficulties an opportunity for growth? (page 68)
   - When you face struggles, what is typically your first response? (page 71)
   - From Proverbs 11:2 (NIV) we read, "When pride comes, then comes disgrace, but with humility comes wisdom." What emotions and feelings come to mind after hearing this verse?

Deeper Conversation (15 minutes)

Divide into smaller groups of two to three for deeper conversation. (Encourage the women to break into different groups each week.) If you'd like, before the session, write on a markerboard or chart paper the following questions. You could also do this in the form of a handout.

- How might living out Jeremiah 29:13 transform your daily walk with God? What might that look like for you?
- Where did you see God at work in your life this past week?

Closing Prayer (5 minutes)

Close the session by taking personal prayer requests from group members and leading the group in prayer. As you progress to later weeks in the study, you might encourage members to participate by praying out loud for one another and the requests given.

3

Action

Living a Life Where Actions Match Faith

LEADER PREP (BEFORE THE SESSION)

Overview

This week we considered that real faith is backed up by action, exploring selected verses in James 1 and 2 as well as additional Scriptures. James teaches us that our actions must match our beliefs, leading us to serve others and make disciples of Jesus Christ. Though we do not earn salvation through good deeds, our good deeds are an outpouring of our salvation and our love for Jesus. We ended the week considering our call to be on mission in the world, living out our faith in real and practical ways.

Memory Verse

Do not merely listen to the word, and so deceive yourselves. Do what it says.

(James 1:22 NIV)

What You Will Need

- *Thrive* DVD and DVD player, or equipment to stream the video online
- Bible and *Thrive* participant workbook for reference
- Markerboard or chart paper and markers (optional)
- Stick-on name tags and markers (optional)
- iPod, smartphone, or tablet and portable speaker (optional)

SESSION OUTLINE

Welcome and Opening Prayer
(5–10 minutes, depending on session length)

In order to create a warm, welcoming environment as the women are gathering before the session begins, consider lighting one or more candles, providing coffee or other refreshments, playing worship music, or all of these. (Bring an iPod, smartphone, or tablet and a portable speaker if desired.) Be sure to provide name tags if the women do not know one

another or you have new participants in your group. Then, when you are ready to begin, open the group in prayer.

If meeting online, welcome each participant as she joins and encourage the women to talk informally until you are ready to open the group in prayer.

Icebreaker (5 minutes)

Invite the women to share a short response to the following question without repeating any of the previous responses:

- What is one way you have put your faith into action?

Video (20 minutes)

Play the Week 3 video segment. Invite participants to complete the Video Viewer Guide for Week 3 in the participant workbook as they watch (page 104).

Group Discussion (25–35 minutes, depending on session length)

Note: More material is provided than you will have time to include. Before the session, select what you want to cover.

VIDEO DISCUSSION QUESTIONS

- The memory verse this week cautions against a "dead faith." What does that mean to you?
- In this session, Jen spoke about being made to know God, to grow in faith and to put that faith into action. Where do you see faith in action? in our church? in the community? in your family?
  - Jen shared a story from her youth where she saw faith in action in a worship service in New York City. Have you had an experience like that when your eyes were open in a new way to faithful action?
  - Faith *without works* is a bad look for the Christian community. Do you see this as well? How does it affect non-Christians' understanding of what it means to follow Jesus?

PARTICIPANT WORKBOOK DISCUSSION QUESTIONS

1. During our Day 1 lesson we were reminded from the book of James that a believer's action must match his or her beliefs. Our Memory Verse, James 1:22, implores us to do what the Bible says.

   - When have you seen someone's faith in action and thought it was a powerful testimony? (page 76)

   - How do you put your faith into action on a weekly basis? (page 76) How does it feel when you put your faith into action by serving others?

   - How does the kingdom suffer when we do not live out our faith in practical ways? (page 78)

   - Ask someone to read aloud James 2:16. As Christ-followers, describe the actions we should take according to this verse.

2. In our Day 2 lesson we were challenged to live out James 2:17. Our faith in God requires us to put our faith into our action and help one another.

   - Think back to a recent time when you needed help. Who helped you and how did it make you feel knowing someone cared to reach out to you?

   - Why is following the Great Commandment essential for Christian living?

   - You know from experience that loving God and loving others isn't always easy. Give a recent example of when acting in love wasn't easy. (page 85)

   - What was the outcome of that experience? What kind of effect did putting your faith into action through love have? (page 86)

3. In our Day 3 lesson we discovered the importance of being disciples of Jesus by sharing the good news with others. We considered that our faith transforms our actions so we may carry out the good news of Jesus.

- Ask someone to read aloud Isaiah 6:8. Does hearing this verse give you pause, empower you to serve, or stir emotions in your heart, or all of these?
- How did you come to know Jesus personally? (page 89)
- Have someone read aloud Matthew 28:16-20 or ask participants to read the verses silently. What did the Son of God say in his final moments with his team? (page 90)
- Sometimes sharing the good news of Jesus is difficult for us. What are some ways you can put your faith into action by reaching out to others using your God-given talents and abilities?

4. On Day 4 we learned that our walk with Christ is a process of becoming a new creation. Our works and actions become an outpouring of the transformation that is occurring in us.
- Reflect on John 14:15 and John 13:35. What does obedience in response to salvation look like? (page 94)
- What specific fruit or traits would you expect to find in the life of a believer who is mature in their faith? (page 95)
- How would you explain to a new believer why we do not earn salvation through our good deeds and actions?
- What are some of your gifts, talents, and abilities? How might you use them to bless others and honor God? (page 96)

5. James knew that for the church to thrive, Christ-followers must be willing to live out their commitment to Jesus. We must be faithful in our worship of God if we are to thrive.
- Reflect on 2 Chronicles 16:9a. What are your thoughts as you imagine God searching the earth to find people who are faithful? (page 100)
- As followers of Christ, we are called to be on mission, yet not all of us who are sent respond willingly. What are some of the reservations or hesitations we see in those who were called in the Bible?

- When has God spoken to you and you responded by making excuses? (page 101)
- Ask someone to read aloud Isaiah 6:8 (NIV). How does hearing this verse move you? What was the last thing God called you to do? What was your response? (page 103)

Deeper Conversation (15 minutes)

Divide into smaller groups of two to three for deeper conversation. (Encourage the women to break into different groups each week.) If you'd like, before the session, write on a markerboard or chart paper the following questions. You could also do this in the form of a handout.

- How has putting your faith into action brought you joy and grown your faith?
- Where did you see God at work in your life this past week?

Closing Prayer (5 minutes)

Close the session by taking personal prayer requests from group members and leading the group in prayer. As you progress to later weeks in the study, you might encourage members to participate by praying out loud for one another and the requests given.

Control

Taming
the Tongue

Session Notes: WEEK 4

_____
_____
_____
_____
_____
_____
_____
_____
_____
_____
_____
_____
_____
_____
_____

LEADER PREP (BEFORE THE SESSION)

Overview

This week we looked to verses in James 1 and 3, as well as additional Scriptures, as we considered the theme of control—specifically, controlling our words. We learned from James that our words reflect our hearts and have tremendous power. Our language has the power to build up and to destroy. So, we must give God control of our mouths so that our words can bring life and hope to others and glory to God. We thrive when we allow our speech to be a blessing to others.

Memory Verse

If you claim to be religious but don't control your tongue, you are fooling yourself, and your religion is worthless.

(James 1:26)

What You Will Need

- *Thrive* DVD and DVD player, or equipment to stream the video online
- Bible and *Thrive* participant workbook for reference
- Markerboard or chart paper and markers (optional)
- Stick-on name tags and markers (optional)
- iPod, smartphone, or tablet and portable speaker (optional)

SESSION OUTLINE

Welcome and Opening Prayer
(5–10 minutes, depending on session length)

In order to create a warm, welcoming environment as the women are gathering before the session begins, consider lighting one or more candles, providing coffee or other refreshments, playing worship music, or all of these. (Bring an iPod, smartphone, or tablet and a portable speaker if desired.) Be sure to provide name tags if the women do not know one another or you have new participants in your group. Then, when you are ready to begin, open the group in prayer.

If meeting online, welcome each participant as she joins and encourage the women to talk informally until you are ready to open the group in prayer.

Icebreaker (5 minutes)

Invite the women to share short responses to the following question:

- When have you spoken carelessly and later regretted it?

Video (20 minutes)

Play the Week 4 video segment. Invite participants to complete the Video Viewer Guide for Week 4 in the participant workbook as they watch (page 133).

Group Discussion (25–35 minutes, depending on session length)

Note: More material is provided than you will have time to include. Before the session, select what you want to cover.

VIDEO DISCUSSION QUESTIONS

- Ask if anyone has experience with horses and can speak to training and to the use of the bit that Jen describes.
- How do you see the difference in "training" and "taming"? How does that apply in this conversation?
- The memory verse, James 1:26, puts a very high level of importance on our words and their ability to heal or hurt. Are there times this past week when you were more aware of your words—spoken, written, or on social media?
- Ephesians 4:29 (ESV) says a believer's words should be good for building up that it "may give grace to those who hear." What words of encouragement "give grace"? Have you experienced that from someone this week?

PARTICIPANT WORKBOOK DISCUSSION QUESTIONS

1. Many times we are careless with the words we use even when others are listening. To live like Jesus, we must guard our tongue and speak to one another with care and love.
   - Ask someone to read aloud James 1:26. How can this verse inform the way we live with others?

- How have careless words impacted you? Share an example or two. (page 109)
- Now, how have encouraging words impacted you? (page 110)
- Read aloud Proverbs 10:19. What warning and instruction do we find in this verse? (page 110)

2. The words we use have the power to build up or destroy others. As Christians we must set worthy examples since others are watching our actions and listening to our words.
   - Read aloud Proverbs 27:6. Who has spoken a hard truth to you? What was your initial reaction? How has it impacted you long-term? (page 114)
   - Ask someone to read Proverbs 30:5-6. How would you rephrase that verse? (page 114)
   - What advice is given in 2 Timothy 2:15? (page 114)

3. In our Day 3 lesson we were encouraged to become more intentional with the language we use. Daily we must ask God for wisdom to be more like Jesus in our words and deeds.
   - When have you recently stumbled in what you said, saying the wrong thing? Whom did it affect? (page 119)
   - In times of stress, how do you tend to react verbally? (page 120)
   - Read aloud Luke 6:45. What can you do to intentionally fill your heart with what is good and pure?
   - Do you have a go-to verse that you quietly quote when you are tempted to use hurtful words? If so, what is it?

4. On Day 4 we saw that our words can be used for good and for harm. Proverbs 18:4 (AMP) reminds us, "The words of a man's mouth are like deep waters [copious and difficult to fathom]; The fountain of [mature, godly] wisdom is like a bubbling stream [sparkling, fresh, pure, and life-giving]." It's important to live like Christ in our speech and actions.
   - Who has spoken words to you that brought healing and encouragement? (page 124)

- When have words torn you down and caused you pain? (page 124)
- When have you witnessed someone using kind and compassionate words that made a difference in a difficult situation?
- Ask someone to read aloud Hebrews 4:12. What feelings arise about your speech after hearing the latter part of this verse?

5. James wanted all his brothers and sisters in Christ to know that words matter. May we use our words to be caring, kind, and compassionate to all we encounter.
   - Describe the atmosphere in your home growing up. (page 129)
   - Ask someone to read aloud Matthew 12:34b. Seeing the atmosphere of your current home through the lens of this verse, what changes need to be made?
   - How did you summarize what James is saying in James 3:9-12? (page 129)
   - Read aloud Psalm 51:10. Describe the right spirit you would like to have in your life.
   - Are you ready to double down on being an encourager? What challenges might you face? (page 131)

Deeper Conversation (15 minutes)

Divide into smaller groups of two to three for deeper conversation. (Encourage the women to break into different groups each week.) If you'd like, before the session, write on a markerboard or chart paper the questions below. You could also do this in the form of a handout.

- What are some ways you can put James 1:19b into action?
- Where did you see God at work in your life this past week?

Closing Prayer (5 minutes)

Close the session by taking personal prayer requests from group members and leading the group in prayer. Encourage members to participate by praying out loud for one another and the requests given.

HUMILITY

Developing the Attitude of Christ

Session Notes: WEEK 5

LEADER PREP (BEFORE THE SESSION)

Overview

This week we explored the theme of humility, reading selected verses from James 2 and 4, along with additional Scriptures. We considered what it means to surrender control and humble ourselves as Christ did, discovering that God responds to humility with grace. From Matthew 5:5 (GNT) we read, "Happy are those who are humble; they will receive what God has promised!" Developing an attitude of humility like Christ requires us to think less of ourselves, seek God, and look to the needs of others. When we humble ourselves before God, serving the Lord and others, we thrive spiritually and experience the life God has promised us.

Memory Verse

So humble yourselves before God. Resist the devil, and he will flee from you.

(James 4:7)

What You Will Need

- *Thrive* DVD and DVD player, or equipment to stream the video online
- Bible and *Thrive* participant workbook for reference
- Markerboard or chart paper and markers (optional)
- Stick-on name tags and markers (optional)
- iPod, smartphone, or tablet and portable speaker (optional)

SESSION OUTLINE

Welcome and Opening Prayer
(5–10 minutes, depending on session length)

In order to create a warm, welcoming environment as the women are gathering before the session begins, consider lighting one or more candles, providing coffee or other refreshments, playing worship music, or all of these. (Bring an iPod, smartphone, or tablet and a portable speaker if desired.) Be sure to provide name tags if the women do not know one

another or you have new participants in your group. Then, when you are ready to begin, open the group in prayer.

If meeting online, welcome each participant as she joins and encourage the women to talk informally until you are ready to open the group in prayer.

Icebreaker (5 minutes)

Invite the women to share short responses to the following question:

- What is a humbling experience you've had?

Video (20 minutes)

Play the Week 5 video segment. Invite participants to complete the Video Viewer Guide for Week 5 in the participant workbook as they watch (page 162).

Group Discussion (25–35 minutes, depending on session length)

Note: More material is provided than you will have time to include. Before the session, select what you want to cover.

Video Discussion Questions

- In the opening vignette, with the ballerinas in training, Jen sees the importance of humility in training to be proficient and excel in something whether it's dance or faithfulness. Is anyone willing to share a time when they learned that the hard way?
- Jen says in this session, "humility is a mark of maturity in character." What are some examples of that in your faith mentors? What do you see in your own life?
- "Humility is not thinking less of yourself, but thinking of yourself less." Unpack the quote from Rick Warren. How can we be both humble and have self-confidence and self-care.
- What biblical character do you think of who exhibits deep humility?
- From the video and the readings, how do you see watching our motives as a way to grow toward greater humility?

PARTICIPANT WORKBOOK DISCUSSION QUESTIONS

1. On Day 1 we delved into the battle of pride versus humility. James felt the need to address humility, pride, and jealousy with the early believers who were living in such a challenging time, and his words are as relevant today as they were then. Humbling ourselves like Christ is a tall order, but there is strength in humility—strength of character, of faith, of relationships, and of conviction.

    *   Read aloud James 4:1-3. What insights do you gather about how pride and jealousy play into our relationships? (page 137)
    *   Have you ever experienced the destructive "fall" that follows pride? Describe it. (page 138)
    *   Ask someone to read aloud Matthew 5:5. What are your thoughts and emotions as you reflect on this verse?
    *   Where might you have wrong motives in your life right now? How might you humble yourself to find peace this week? (page 139)

2. On Day 2 we saw that humility is putting the needs of others ahead of your own, even if you aren't treated with kindness in the process. James reminds us to imitate the humility of Christ.

    *   When have you had to humble yourself to serve someone? (page 142)
    *   Ask someone to read aloud James 4:6-7. When have you seen God oppose the proud and give grace to the humble? Why do you think God does this?
    *   Reflect on an experience when you went out of your way to help another, yet no thanks were given for your efforts. Describe the feelings you had.
    *   How can you imitate Christ in serving others this week? (page 144)

3. At first glance the words of warning in James 4:4-7 seem harsh. But as we learn on Day 3, God desires us to humble ourselves so that we may prioritize God's desires and be faithful.

   - Share your thoughts in response to this statement: James is clear: we cannot love and serve God and love and serve the values of this world at the same time.
   - James 4:7 has both a premise and a promise. The premise is what must be met in order to receive or claim the promise. What is the premise of this verse? What is the promise? (page 148)
   - How does putting aside our agenda to embrace God's agenda help us to practice humility? As you are willing, share an example from your own life.

4. On Day 4 we discovered a wonderful way to thrive through humility: to admit where we need to repent in order to become the most Christlike version of ourselves. When we confront areas of sin and repent, God lifts us up in honor.

   - What keeps you from drawing close to God on a regular basis? (page 152)
   - What safeguards can you put in place to be focused on staying close to Jesus? (page 153)
   - Ask someone to read aloud Psalm 139:23-24. What is God teaching us through these verses?
   - What are your spiritual habits? How effective have those habits been recently in bringing growth? What needs attention? (page 153)

5. In the last lesson of the week, we looked to chapter 2 and considered James's words about favoritism, which at its core is also about humility. A humble spirit shows no partiality.

   - When has someone humbled themselves to serve you? How did it make you feel? (page 158)
   - Read aloud James 2:1. Who is not to show favoritism? How would you define favoritism? (page 158)

- Share your thoughts and feelings concerning this statement: *favoritism is a sin.*
- Ask someone to read Philippians 2:3 aloud. Why is it vital to put the needs of others first?

Deeper Conversation (15 minutes)

Divide into smaller groups of two to three for deeper conversation. (Encourage the women to break into different groups each week.) If you'd like, before the session, write on a markerboard or chart paper the questions below. You could also do this in the form of a handout.

- How have favoritism and prejudice affected you personally? (page 160) What did you discover from your experience(s)?
- Where did you see God at work in your life this past week?

Closing Prayer (5 minutes)

Close the session by taking personal prayer requests from group members and leading the group in prayer. Encourage members to participate by praying out loud for one another and the requests given.

PRAYER

Exercising the Power Tool of the Faith

LEADER PREP (BEFORE THE SESSION)

Overview

This week we explored the theme of prayer in James 5, along with additional Scriptures. What a comfort it is to know that we can call out to God any moment of the day! Sometimes we get caught up in the correct language we should use or the correct posture to have as we pray, but God simply desires a relationship with us and is eager for us to call out to Him in joy and in sorrow. Through prayer we strengthen our relationship with God as we tell God about what is happening in our lives, share our needs, confess our sins, and pray for others. To thrive in our Christian journey, we must exercise the power tool of faith—that of prayer.

Memory Verse

The earnest prayer of a righteous person has great power and produces wonderful results.

(James 5:16b)

What You Will Need

- *Thrive* DVD and DVD player, or equipment to stream the video online
- Bible and *Thrive* participant workbook for reference
- Markerboard or chart paper and markers (optional)
- Stick-on name tags and markers (optional)
- iPod, smartphone, or tablet and portable speaker (optional)

SESSION OUTLINE

Welcome and Opening Prayer
(5–10 minutes, depending on session length)

In order to create a warm, welcoming environment as the women are gathering before the session begins, consider lighting one or more candles, providing coffee or other refreshments, playing worship music, or all of these. (Bring an iPod, smartphone, or tablet and a portable speaker if

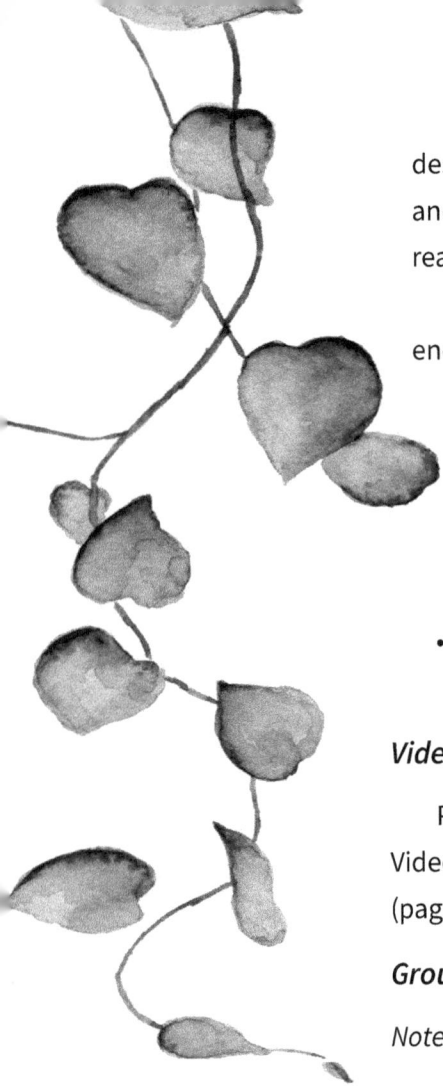

desired.) Be sure to provide name tags if the women do not know one another or you have new participants in your group. Then, when you are ready to begin, open the group in prayer.

If meeting online, welcome each participant as she joins and encourage the women to talk informally until you are ready to open the group in prayer.

Icebreaker (5 minutes)

Invite the women to share short responses to the following question:

- What was the earliest spoken prayer you were introduced to as a child?

Video (20 minutes)

Play the Week 6 video segment. Invite participants to complete the Video Viewer Guide for Week 6 in the participant workbook as they watch (page 194).

Group Discussion (25–35 minutes, depending on session length)

Note: More material is provided than you will have time to include. Before the session, select what you want to cover.

VIDEO DISCUSSION QUESTIONS

- What parallels did you see in the example of the greenhouse Jen visited and your daily Christian life?
- What was your childhood experience of prayer? How did you learn to pray?
- Jen mentions a friend who didn't think that her prayers were "good." What do you think it means to pray well?
- The second tip Jen talks about is to be faithful in prayer. What are ways that we can pray in accordance with God's will? Has this changed for you as you have grown in faith?

1. On Day 1 we considered that prayer is both talking and listening to God. How many times a day or week do you talk with a friend? Now think of God as a friend. Do you talk with God as many times as you talk with your friends? God loves hearing from us and wants us to pray about everything and anything.

   - Is praying a difficult or an easy practice for you? Share why.
   - Ask someone to read aloud Matthew 27:50-51. What happened when Jesus died on the cross? (page 168)
   - Read James 5:13. When and what does James say we are to pray? (page 169)

2. On Day 2 we began an exploration of what it means to pray without ceasing. God loves us so much and wants to stay in constant communication with us.

   - How would you describe what it means to pray without ceasing?
   - What struggles have you had in your prayer journey? (page 172)
   - What victories have you experienced through prayer? (page 172)
   - Ask someone to read aloud Luke 22:42. What did Jesus pray as He faced death on the cross? (page 172)

3. On Day 3 we considered times and postures for prayer. Both James and Paul encourage us to pray at all times about all things. And in Psalm 95:6 (NIV) we find an invitation to pray on our knees, "Come, let us bow down in worship, let us kneel before the Lord our Maker."

   - How does it comfort you to know that God is eager to meet with you at any moment? (page 176)
   - In Ephesians 6:10-13 Paul describes spiritual armor. Name the pieces of the armor of God. What instruction does Paul give in verse 18? (page 177)

- If you are physically able to kneel, how does this posture help you to humble yourself before the Lord? If you are physically unable to kneel, what are some other postures and ways you can take a position of humility before the Lord? (page 179)
- Respond to this statement: Prayer is one of the greatest gifts God has given us.

4. On Day 4 we explored how to pray effectively and develop a powerful life of prayer. In the Lord's Prayer we find the key elements of prayer.
   - Ask someone to read aloud James 5:16. According to James, what brings powerful and wonderful results in prayer? (page 182)
   - When have you cried out to God with an honest, earnest prayer? How did God respond? (page 183)
   - When did you learn the Lord's Prayer? How has it helped you in your Christian journey and, specifically, in your prayer life?
   - Invite participants to share their versions of the Lord's Prayer (page 186). Then say the Lord's Prayer together.

5. In his quest for believers to follow the example of Jesus, James gives us a command in the final chapter of his book to do the hard work of faith. On Day 5 we explored James's call to prayer that ends with a call to the actions of confession and restoration.
   - "Confess your sins to each other" (James 5:16). What thoughts and emotions do you have when you hear this statement? (page 189)
     - Who in your life has demonstrated real love by doing the hard thing on your behalf? (page 192)
       - Think of friends or relatives who have wandered away from God. If you are willing to reach out to them, what is your plan of action? Share any hesitancies or concerns. What is God's invitation? (pages 192–193)

- Read aloud James 5:16-20. What words or phrases stand out or call to you? How do they speak to you?

Deeper Conversation (15 minutes)

Divide into smaller groups of two to three for deeper conversation. (Encourage the women to break into different groups each week.) If you'd like, before the session, write on a markerboard or chart paper the questions below. You could also do this in the form of a handout.

- Where did you see God at work in your life this past week?
- How have these lessons equipped you to thrive?

Closing Prayer (5 minutes)

Close the session by taking personal prayer requests from group members and leading the group in prayer. Encourage members to participate by praying out loud for one another and the requests given.

Video Viewer Guide: ANSWERS

Week 1

thrive / prospering / flourishing

prepare

if / when

Week 2

grow older / growing up

separates

Wisdom

draw close

do

Week 3

Possible answers for blanks 1–3:
Each created for a unique purpose /
work together / productive / help the
world around them thrive / produce
something wonderful.

action

faithful / good deeds

Week 4

Decide

Immerse

Ask

Week 5

less / but / less

examine

Humble

Resist

Week 6

sincere

faithful

relentless

sincere / faithful / relentless /
change / world

Group Roster

Name	Phone	Email

More Bible Studies from Jennifer Cowart

Learn from the fierce women of God who changed the world.

Fierce: Women of the Bible Who Changed the World

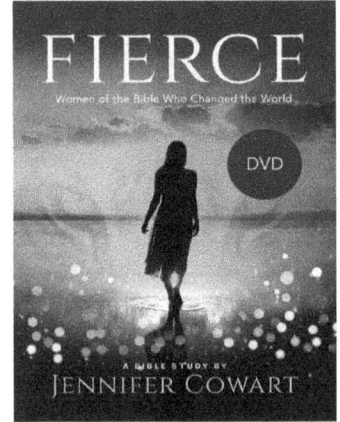

The word *fierce* is trendy. It is used to describe women who are extreme athletes, high-level executives, or supermodels. Women at the top of their game. But what about the rest of us? Can we be fierce? Absolutely! In fact, women like us have been changing the world for thousands of years—many who received little fanfare yet lived fiercely anyway. In this six-week study we will look at lesser-known female characters in the Bible and the ways they changed the world by living into God's calling, including:

- The midwives of Egypt (Shiphrah and Puah), who made hard decisions in the face of evil
- Deborah, who was an unlikely and powerful leader
- Naaman's slave girl, who bravely points others to God's healing power
- The Woman at the Well, who boldly repented and shared her faith
- Lois and Eunice, who parented with intentionality and effectiveness
- Dorcas, who showed kindness to those in need.

As we explore their lives, we will discover how we too can live into our callings, honor the Lord, and even change the world through our courage, faithfulness, and obedience.

Explore excerpts and video teaching samples at AbingdonWomen.com.

Abingdon *Women*

More Bible Studies from Jennifer Cowart

God can turn your messy life into a masterpiece.
Messy People: Life Lessons from Imperfect Biblical Heroes

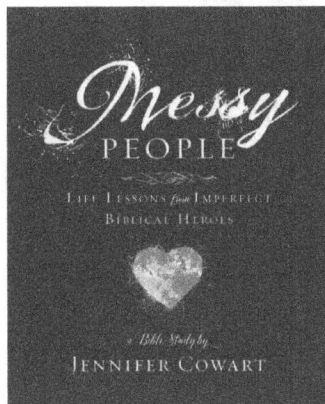

Participant Workbook | 9781501863127

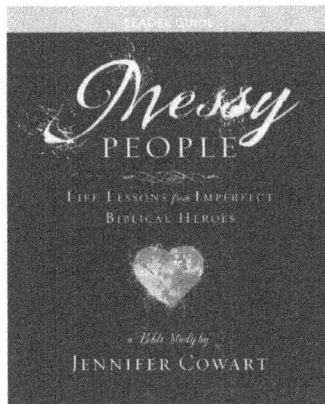

Leader Guide | 9781501863141

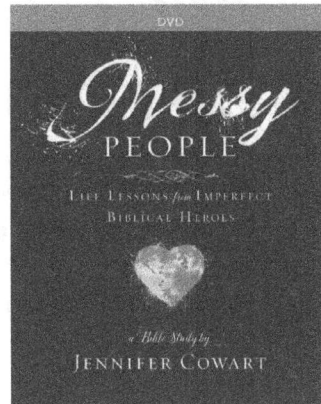

Video-DVD | 9781501863165

Every life gets messy at times. Sometimes these messes are literal, like a house that would be easier to condemn than to clean. But sometimes they are intangible messes such as illness, conflict, depression, abuse, bankruptcy, divorce, and job loss. And these messes can be painful, hurting our hearts and our homes. But as we see in the Bible, God loves to use messy people!

In this six-week study, we will dig into the lives of biblical heroes who were messy people just like us but who were used by God in powerful ways.

Together we will examine the stories of five wonderful but messy people and one messy parable character:

- Rahab
- The Prodigal Son
- Josiah
- Mary
- David
- Daniel

From their stories, we will learn how God can use broken people, restore damaged hearts and relationships, give us power to handle our critics, and help us deal with the hard moments of life. Along the way we'll discover that we don't have to just endure messy lives but can actually learn to thrive with God's guidance and help. In the hands of God, our messes can become His masterpieces!

Explore excerpts and video teaching samples at AbingdonWomen.com.

Abingdon *Women*

WATCH VIDEOS BASED ON

THRIVE:

LIVING FAITHFULLY IN DIFFICULT TIMES
WITH JENNIFER COWART THROUGH AMPLIFY MEDIA.

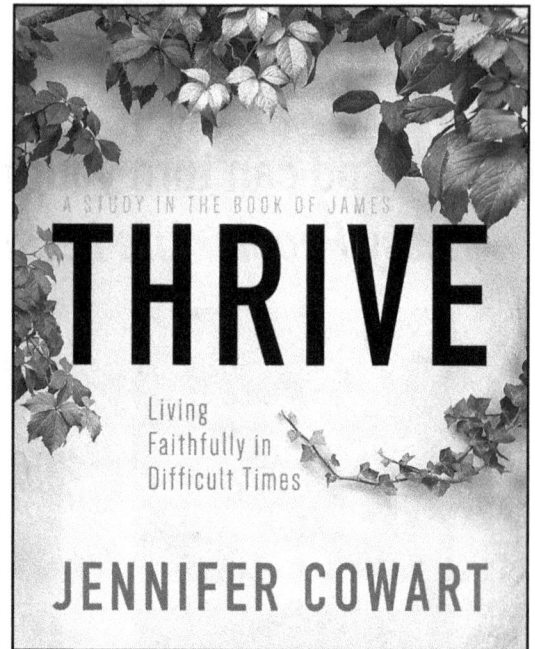

Amplify Media is a multimedia platform that delivers high-quality, searchable content with an emphasis on Wesleyan perspectives for churchwide, group, or individual use on any device at any time. In a world of sometimes overwhelming choices, Amplify gives church leaders and congregants media capabilities that are contemporary, relevant, effective, and, most important, affordable and sustainable.

With *Amplify Media* church leaders can:

- Provide a reliable source of Christian content through a Wesleyan lens for teaching, training, and inspiration in a customizable library
- Deliver their own preaching and worship content in a way the congregation knows and appreciates
- Build the church's capacity to innovate with engaging content and accessible technology
- Equip the congregation to better understand the Bible and its application
- Deepen discipleship beyond the church walls

⋀ AMPLIFY. MEDIA

Ask your group leader or pastor about Amplify Media and sign up today at www.AmplifyMedia.com.

www.ingramcontent.com/pod-product-compliance
Lightning Source LLC
Chambersburg PA
CBHW081137090426
42737CB00018B/3353